Original title:
Paradise on the Horizon

Copyright © 2025 Creative Arts Management OÜ
All rights reserved.

Author: Colin Leclair
ISBN HARDBACK: 978-1-80581-656-0
ISBN PAPERBACK: 978-1-80581-183-1
ISBN EBOOK: 978-1-80581-656-0

Visions of Tranquil Heights

I climbed a tree to see the view,
But got stuck like a cat in a shoe.
The daisies giggled, the sun turned red,
As squirrels debated what I should be fed.

Clouds rolled by like fluffy boats,
While birds had meetings, plotting their hoax.
I waved to the sun, it winked back with glee,
Saying, 'Stay up here, it's quite fun, you see!'

Whispers Underneath the Evening Star

The moon wore shades and danced on a beam,
While crickets held a midnight ice cream dream.
The fireflies twinkled, lighting the way,
Saying, 'Come join our disco, don't miss the sway!'

The stars shared secrets, tickled the night,
As frogs in tuxedos leaped left and right.
Laughter echoed across the cool grass,
As dreams bounced around like a jolly jackass.

The Land Where Hearts Flourish

In fields of candy, the cows wore hats,
While butterflies argued over friendly chats.
The flowers wore smiles, all bright and loud,
Claiming to be the best in the crowd.

Wishing wells whispered, 'Throw us some change!'
While gnomes played poker, a little deranged.
With rainbows for slides and clouds for swings,
This land had a charm only laughter brings.

Where Watercolors Meet the Sky

The sunset splashed colors like a child's art,
With paints spilled over, but that's just the start.
The ocean giggled, tickling the shore,
As waves tried to skate, but ended up poor.

Seagulls debated their next great dive,
'This sandwich is mine!' they'd argue and strive.
While sunflowers danced to the breeze's sweet tunes,
This world of splendor was painted by loons.

Gleaming Fields of Tomorrow

In fields where cows wear shades of cool,
The grass grows high, it's nature's rule.
Sunflowers dance to the gardener's tune,
While rabbits plot under the bright moon.

A pie tastes better with a pinch of sun,
And we make lemonade, just for fun.
Squirrels debate over who looks best,
In this goofy nature, we can jest.

Secrets in the Twilight Glow

Under stars that giggle in the night,
We find the critters, oh what a sight.
The moon, a whisperer, shares tales wide,
While owls hoot and squirrels take a ride.

Each tree holds secrets, squirrelly and bright,
As we uncover truths in the fading light.
The shadows may chuckle as we stomp and sway,
In this whimsical dance, we lose our way.

The Allure of Star-Kissed Sands

On beaches where the sand tickles our feet,
Crabs hold a dance-off, a funny retreat.
Seagulls squawk jokes, diving for fries,
While mermaids giggle, wearing seaweed ties.

With castles of shells that fall with a gust,
We laugh at the waves, in sunshine we trust.
Flip-flops fly off in the salty breeze,
As we chase our laughter, doing as we please.

Resplendent Oasis Awaiting

Among palm trees where the otters swim,
There's a guy in a sunhat who sings like a hymn.
Coconuts chuckle, rolling on the ground,
While lizards lounge as if they own the town.

The hammock sways low, a slack-line pro,
It's a race with the breeze, and here we go!
Sips of coconut water, icy and sweet,
In this kooky haven, life's a fun treat.

Lifting the Veil of Serene Mystique

Dreams stumble like puppies in the grass,
Chasing butterflies that are made of sass.
Laughter echoes where the sunbeam meets,
Tickling toes and dancing in fleets.

Mystique lifts with a wink and a cheer,
A monkey on a beach ball, drawing near.
Jokes unravel like ribbons in air,
As seagulls squawk in a comical flare.

Where Hope Blooms in Twilight

In twilight's glow, the fireflies play,
We race to catch them, oh what a display!
With pockets aflutter, we laugh and we prance,
Each glowing creature sparks a new dance.

Hope blooms brightly in laughter's sweet sound,
A stitch in time, where silliness found.
Silly hats and mismatched shoes,
In this glowing realm, we can't lose!

The Call of Timeless Places

Oh, the places we'll go on this silly spree,
Where tigers ride bikes, maybe even a bee.
With waffles that sing and run down the street,
Every corner holds wonders, oh how they greet!

In timeless giggles, we sail on a cloud,
With a cuckoo clock laughing, oh so loud.
Sailing on donuts, we won't lose our way,
In this realm of the wacky, let's frolic and play!

Reflections in Amber Tides

Waves whisper tales and tickle our feet,
With jellybeans dancing, life's sugary treat.
Mirrors of laughter reflect from the shore,
As seaweed performs, we beg for encore!

Amber tides bubble with giggles galore,
Shells trade their secrets, we can't help but roar.
In this sparkling world where whimsy collides,
We dip our toes in, where mirth never hides.

The Lure of Forgotten Realms

In a land where socks are lost,
And laundry baskets reign supreme,
There's a castle made of marshmallows,
Where gummy bears live the sweetest dream.

A river flows with fizzy drink,
And candy fish swim all around,
The trees are really lollipops,
This realm of fun is truly found.

You'd think the king would rule with grace,
But he's busy devouring pie,
While jester ducks quack punchlines loud,
And the court laughs 'til they cry.

So pack your bags and jump on in,
Forget the chores, let laughter ring,
In this land of joy and whimsy,
It's where the silly dreams take wing.

Symphony of the Looming Light

When the sun does dance at dawn,
And coffee sings a happy tune,
The cereal waves like pop stars,
In a breakfast bowl beneath the moon.

With waffle boats on syrup streams,
And butter clouds that float so high,
The pancakes flip like acrobats,
While toast takes wing and starts to fly.

The whispers of the morning breeze,
Could make a grumpy cat take flight,
As soloists of muffins rise,
In this symphony of pure delight.

So tune your heart to golden rays,
And let the breakfast bliss commence,
With every bite, a world of joy,
Where laughter reigns in every sense.

Beyond the Fading Twilight

As the stars put on their dance shoes,
And moonlight struts across the sky,
The fireflies hold a glow stick rave,
While owls hoot their party cry.

Beneath the trees with candy canes,
The marshmallow bunnies hop around,
They trade their secrets with the ants,
In this twilight magic, joy is found.

The crickets play a jazzy tune,
As twilight wraps the world in fun,
The laughter echoes through the night,
A chorus 'neath the setting sun.

So raise a glass of silly dreams,
Join in the dance of cosmic cheer,
Beyond the fading of the light,
Is where your heart learns how to steer.

Soaring into Endless Blue

On a hot air balloon of giggles,
We float above a sea of cheese,
With birds that wear a jaunty hat,
And planes that tickle with the breeze.

The clouds are made of whipped cream swirls,
While rain drops drop like jelly beans,
We bounce on skies of cotton fluff,
Chasing all our wildest dreams.

With ice cream cones as mountain peaks,
And rivers filled with lemonade,
We'll sail through skies of silly fun,
Grinning wide as joys cascade.

So grab a spoon and take a leap,
Into this sky of endless hue,
For in this flight of laughter's grace,
We find a world that's bright and new.

A Search Through the Timeless Sea

In a boat made of marshmallows so sweet,
I searched for treasure, oh what a treat!
Fish wore hats and danced on the waves,
While I hummed a tune through salty caves.

Seagulls squawked, mischief in the air,
Stealing snacks, they just didn't care!
A crab in a tuxedo shuffled by,
With a wink and a nod, he gave a sly high.

The sun wore sunglasses, looking so cool,
As I splashed around in a jellybean pool.
Shells giggled, whispered secrets of old,
While dolphins in tuxedos danced bold.

At last, I found a chest filled with jelly,
But when I opened it, I felt quite smelly!
Rubber ducks floated, laughing with glee,
In my timeless quest across the sea!

The Secret Garden of Dreams

In a garden where flowers could talk,
They played hopscotch and took a long walk.
Bees wore glasses, sipping sweet tea,
While leaves giggled, 'Oh, such a spree!'

A cat with a monocle read a book,
Sharing tales that no one would cook.
Toadstools danced with an air of delight,
As fireflies played tag, blinking light.

The sun wore a crown, oh what a sight,
While clouds played hide and seek in their flight.
Every petal shared jokes, oh so fine,
As I giggled along, sipping on thyme.

A rabbit in sneakers did flips and rolls,
As laughter erupted from all the holes.
In this garden where dreams spun around,
The flashiest fun was endlessly found!

Where Lighthouses Guide the Heart

Beneath a sky painted with giggles and dreams,
A lighthouse flashed signals to all teams.
Waves wearing glasses splashed with cheer,
As sandcastles shouted, 'We have no fear!'

A whale with a trumpet played tunes from the blue,
While seahorses waltzed in their shiny new queue.
"Oh, look at us!" did the barnacles boast,
As crabs in threadbare suits raised their toast.

The moon rolled in, sporting a cheeky grin,
As stars threw confetti, letting the fun begin.
With lanterns bobbing like jelly-filled dreams,
We danced on the shore to the light of moonbeams.

So here's to the lighthouses ready to steer,
With laughter as bright as the stars in the sphere.
In this quirky world where the heart finds its beat,
We revel together, oh what a treat!

Glimmering Shores of Mai

Sand in my sandwich, oh what a treat,
Seagulls are laughing, dancing on heat.
I shout at a crab, 'You're stealing my fries!'
He just waves his claws, with a wink in his eyes.

Shells full of secrets, treasures galore,
One holds a tune that makes mermaids snore.
I stumble and tumble, right into a wave,
The ocean just chuckles, my bravery's brave!

Sunrises Beyond the Veil

The rooster's confused, calls at the moon,
I sip my coffee, taste of cartoon.
The sun starts to giggle, peeking awake,
Brushing off clouds like icing on cake.

Birds on the beach throw a feathered parade,
They dance like they're bold, hope I'm not made.
I laugh as they dive, a wild feather fight,
As I sip my drink, all the world's feeling right.

When Oceans Flirt with the Dawn

Waves flirt with sand, a cheeky old game,
They kiss and retreat, never staying the same.
Seagulls on surfboards, riding with glee,
I join in the fun, it's as wild as can be!

The sun winks at dolphins that splash with delight,
As I roll in the waves, with a flip and a flight.
The ocean declares, 'Hey, you're one of us!'
But I splash back, 'Just here for the fuss!'

Tides of Tranquil Trust

The tide whispers secrets in a low, merry voice,
Telling old tales of a fish and his choice.
'Why did you leave?' asks a clam with a pout,
'I wanted adventure!' the fish bits out.

I bask in the sun, a towel my throne,
While crabs play charades, a haphazard show.
There's laughter in the breeze, a joy without bounds,
As the beach becomes home, where silliness surrounds.

Reflections of the Boundless Sky

Up above, the clouds parade,
Wearing hats that never fade.
A flock of ducks with roller skates,
On a trampoline, they levitate.

Rainbows slip on banana peels,
Giggling stars, their laughter feels.
As the sun juggles with the moon,
A cosmic ballet, a silly tune.

Kites that dance like wild-haired sheep,
In the breeze, their secrets keep.
The sun winks, the world spins around,
A circus up there, joy abound!

Glistening Veil of Dusk

The twilight wears a sparkly gown,
With fireflies, it twirls a crown.
Crickets chirp, doing the twist,
While sleepy owls can't resist.

Moonbeams dripping off the trees,
Tickling a slumbering bee's knees.
A cat wearing shades joins the fun,
As shadows stretch, the day is done.

Stars drop marbles, a cosmic game,
Laughter echoes; who's to blame?
The night unfolds like a playful quilt,
In the chaos, dreams are built.

Sketches Beneath the Cosmos

Beneath the stars, a canvas sprawls,
With squiggly lines and silly balls.
A comet slips on cosmic ice,
Drawing doodles, oh so nice!

Aliens sip on milky shakes,
While planets dance, doing breaks.
A rocket pops confetti bright,
In the clutter, pure delight!

Jupiter pranks with stormy jest,
While Saturn spins in a golden vest.
The cosmos hums a playful tune,
In the art of night, we swoon.

The Allure of Selkie Tides

Selkies frolic in the foam,
With rubber ducks, they make a home.
Waves that tickle, giggles galore,
As they surf the sandy shore.

A seal in shades catches rays,
Sipping lunch on sunny days.
Each splash holds a secret grin,
Our ocean friends, where do we begin?

Mermaids stuck in a seaweed twist,
Searching for their lost fish mist.
The tides roll in, a splashy cheer,
In the water, merriment's near!

Uplifted by the Whispering Breeze

A zephyr whispers quirky jokes,
Tickling the trees, they jolt and poke.
The sun is winking, a playful glow,
As clouds engage in a fluffy show.

Silly seagulls squawk in flight,
Dancing shadows in sheer delight.
The waves clap hands, a salty cheer,
While crabs conspire, spreading good cheer.

Dandelions play tag with the breeze,
While laughter drips from the buzzing bees.
A kite swoops down for a small embrace,
Happy hearts skip in a merry race.

In this space where giggles roam free,
Every laugh joins in a symphony.
With each soft gust, the silliness flows,
In the realm where joy's river glows.

Horizon's Dance of Serenity

A horizon where the colors collide,
Dancing waves take laughter in stride.
Sunset paints quirky with each brush stroke,
While yellows and pinks play hide and poke.

Beach balls bounce with a mind of their own,
While flip-flops tango, high knees are grown.
Sandcastles giggle, merrily tall,
As sea-foam tickles, nature's own call.

The gulls wear sunglasses, stylish and bright,
Commentating tides with all of their might.
Smooth seas whisper puns soft as a dream,
As we sip lemonade, laughter's the theme.

Lollipops sprout from the shore of delight,
While jellyfish mime in the fading light.
In this dance of joy, all worries dissolve,
Each moment's a puzzle, together we solve.

A Voyage Within the Shimmering Dreams

In dreams, we sail on jelly-bean boats,
A sea of giggles as each child floats.
Mermaids sporting top hats take a spin,
While dolphins dance with a toothy grin.

Cotton candy clouds fluff up the sky,
While bubblegum breezes flutter by.
Turtles in tuxedos float like they're grand,
Waving their flippers, a suave little band.

Moonbeams play checkers with bright, shiny stars,
While planets hum tunes from old guitars.
The night sky chuckles, tickling our noses,
As laughter blooms like the sweetest roses.

Adventures swirl in each magical way,
With laughter leading us in the fray.
In this dreamscape, where wishes collide,
Silliness hugs us, a comforting guide.

The Land Where Time Slows Down

In a land where clocks wear a silly grin,
Hiccups of time with laughter begin.
Pine trees giggle as they sway with ease,
While squirrels juggle acorns with glee.

Horses on bicycles race down the lane,
Cheering for rainbows with manifold mane.
Fields of daisies dance side by side,
As butterflies twirl in a giddy glide.

Picnics spread cheer with sandwiches stacked,
As ants on parade wear little backpacks.
Lemonade springs with a fizzy delight,
While shadows laugh in the day's fading light.

Here in this land where humor is king,
Every moment's a bright and silly fling.
With joy as our compass, we twirl and spin,
In this timeless treasure, let laughter begin.

Wishing Well of the Underworld

Down in the depths where the lost socks go,
A coin's splash makes the demons glow.
They wish for snacks and a bit of sun,
Yet they end up with a pack of gum!

The goblins grumble, they want a feast,
But only find lizards, not at all least.
Throw in a nickel for good measure,
And you might just summon a real treasure!

They seek a dance in the middle of night,
But trip on shadows and get such a fright.
With each wish granted, a new twist bends,
Here's to the underworld's laughable trends!

So if you're down and feeling quite blue,
Throw in your worries, let them get skewed.
For even beneath where the dark critters dwell,
You might just find fun in the wishing well!

Traces of Tomorrow's Glow

In dreams of the night, we shed our old plight,
As silly shadows start a dance in the light.
They twist and twirl with a wink and a grin,
Chasing the dawn, let the foolishness begin!

The sun peeks up, and the cats chase their tails,
Silly adventures where laughter prevails.
Flying pancakes on a buttery breeze,
Joyfully juggling with all of the cheese!

Strange creatures join in, with shoes on their heads,
Tapping their toes while they dance on their beds.
Running away from the barking of dreams,
They plot for the day with their whimsical schemes!

So gather your giggles in bundles to throw,
For tomorrow's light is a fab show, you know!
With each hearty chuckle, the world starts to glow,
Leaving traces of laughter as we go with the flow!

The Mutable Nature of Delight

A wiggly worm in a top hat sits high,
Sipping his tea while he tries to fly by.
He muses on laughter, the joy it can bring,
As he waits for the moon to join in the swing!

Frogs on pogo sticks leap with a cheer,
Croaking "Hip-hop!" as they bounce without fear.
They dance with the stars, all frills and all flair,
Wanting to catch just a whiff of the air!

Clouds turn into bunnies, then fanciful bears,
All prancing around in imaginary squares.
Delight's in the movement, as silliness reigns,
Take off those shoes; let's dance in the rains!

So stretch out your arms and just let yourself be,
For delight is mutable, wild, and quite free!
In each quirky moment, let laughter ignite,
For the world seems more fun in the soft morning light!

Sails Set for the Unknown

A boat made of bread sets sail on the blue,
With jellyfish crew and a seagull or two.
They navigate rivers of syrup and cream,
Chasing the sunset, it feels like a dream!

The waves laugh and bubble, tickling the sides,
As fish in tuxedos join in for the rides.
With sandwiches flying and cookies that sing,
Life is a carnival—let the fun fling!

With each gust that puffs and takes off the crust,
The journey is silly, just follow your lust.
For what lies ahead is a mystery so grand,
Set sails for the laughter; this is the plan!

So gather your friends, let the giggles unfold,
A wacky adventure still waiting to be told.
With bread in the water, we glide with a cheer,
On this craft of absurdity, let's disappear!

The Serene Path to Tomorrow

In shoes too tight, we march along,
Chasing dreams that sound like a song.
With giggles loud and fumbles near,
Who knew the sun could bring such cheer?

A squirrel steals our picnic feast,
While we complain, a funny beast!
A dance of crumbs, a laugh so wide,
Tomorrow's troubles, we'll just slide.

The path is bumpy, we trip and sway,
But laughter leads us, come what may.
With silly hats and wild hair,
We strut our stuff without a care.

By dusk we flop, our faces bright,
Dreams of joy in the fading light.
Tomorrow's bound to bring some fun,
So let's just laugh until we're done.

Melodies of the Rising Tide

Waves are crashing, watch them glide,
Seagulls cawing, oh what a ride!
We wade in water, shoes in hand,
Splashing about, it's pretty grand!

A crab does a jig, so out of place,
While we giggle at his silly face.
With every wave, we hop and cheer,
Making memories, oh so dear!

The tide rolls in like a clumsy clown,
Pretending to wear a sparkling crown.
We toss our hats, they float away,
And laugh aloud at our crazy play.

With sunscreen smeared, we look quite bright,
Not quite a model, but what a sight!
The sun dips low, the night's our guide,
Together we'll dream, with the rising tide.

A Glimpse of Otherworldly Bliss

In a world where cupcakes rain from above,
And sprinkles fall like stars we love.
We bounce on clouds, so fluffy and light,
Chasing giggles into the night.

A llama in pajamas strolls by,
With a wink and a grin, oh my, oh my!
He offers us candy with every step,
In this bliss, how can we forget?

The sun wears shades, how chic, how grand,
While we dance like no one's planned.
Frogs in tuxedos sing out a tune,
As we twirl beneath a silly moon.

With every laugh, more joy takes flight,
In a land where wrong feels totally right.
We'll chase the stars on laughter's wings,
In this bliss, oh, how the heart sings!

Under a Canopy of Stars

We lay on grass with popcorn skies,
Counting stars and dreaming high.
A comet zooms past with a wink,
"Is it just me, or did you blink?"

A squirrel debates a peanut prize,
With just the right amount of surprise.
As giggles dance on evening air,
We craft our wishes, floating fair.

Jellybeans tumble from the trees,
Catching them is quite a breeze.
With marshmallow clouds that bounce and sway,
We'll laugh until the break of day.

As midnight strikes, we feign our sleeps,
But laughter bubbles, and joy leaps.
Under this canvas, wild and free,
We find our fun in nonsense glee!

Glistening Pathways to Utopia

On bright paths of jellybeans they tread,
Wearing hats of cheese, they dance ahead.
With rainbows sprouting from their shoes,
They skip along, spreading silly news.

Every tree has candy fruits that swing,
Playing hopscotch with a flying king.
The clouds are made of cotton candy fluff,
While silly giggles are never tough.

In this land where socks are worn on hands,
Lemonade rivers flow, laughter expands.
Worms in tuxedos hold a grand parade,
And happiness is the only trade.

So, come and lose your frowns and woes,
In a world where comedy always flows.
With each step, find joy in life's games,
And remember: nothing's quite the same!

Where Dreams Dance on Air

In a valley where the hedgehogs prance,
Socks in tandem with chips do a dance.
Cats wear glasses and speak like wise owls,
While the bumblebees all sport bright towels.

Jumping clowns on pogo sticks zoom,
Creating a whirlpool of blissful boom.
Up in the sky, fish fly in a spin,
And squirrels plot their nut-thief win.

The sun winks down and wears a fine hat,
Pandas discuss all the latest chit-chat.
With a tickle fight breaking every rule,
The joys of this place make it a jewel.

So frolic along the giddy streams,
Chase after your wildest dreams.
In a laughter-filled land, oh what a ride,
With delightful quirks at every side!

In Search of the Infinite Horizon

On a quest for a land where giggles thrive,
Where pineapples wear shoes and bees can jive.
Each step bounces on a trampoline street,
With hiccups of joy that can't be beat.

A parade of turtles with disco lights,
Swinging their tails to fantastical sights.
Monkeys in tuxedos serve fruity pies,
While dragons sing opera in strange disguise.

The breeze whispers secrets of silly delight,
As kangaroos bounce in sheer delight.
In this world where nonsense reigns supreme,
Forget all your troubles and dive in the dream.

With laughter sprouting from every nook,
Join the wild dance in this nonsensical book.
For in this adrenaline-filled chase,
Laughter is the key to this whimsy space!

Lullabies of the Soft Winds

Beneath a sky of marshmallow clouds,
Frogs sing softly, drawing giggling crowds.
A cheerful breeze hums a lullaby song,
As playgrounds filled with joy stretch wide and long.

Balloons bob along with wobbly grace,
Chasing after rubber ducks in a race.
Cookies dance in circles, soft and sweet,
While the sun plays peek-a-boo in the heat.

Whimsical whispers float through the trees,
Tickling the daisies, carried by ease.
Every corner holds a new delight,
As laughter wraps 'round like stars at night.

So grab a friend, let the fun never end,
With trails of joy that twist and bend.
In a world of smiles that never hide,
Let the shenanigans be your guide!

Harbor of Infinite Possibilities

In a boat built of candy, we set sail,
Chasing dreams that twinkle and never pale.
We pass islands made of ice cream and fries,
With jellybean dolphins that leap through the skies.

Sailing past shores of endless delight,
Where giggles are stars that burst in the night.
The sea's lemonade, refreshing and bright,
Brings laughter to sailors who dance in the light.

Mermaids tell jokes that make sailors snort,
While unicorns play bingo at their favorite port.
With every cheeky wave that the ocean sends,
We're left in stitches, with seaweed as friends.

So let's toast to breezes that tickle and tease,
In a harbor where life is a bowl full of cheese.
With laughter as our anchor and joy as our guide,
We'll sail through the humor of life's joyful tide.

Enchantment in the Soft Glow

In a forest where lightbulbs grow on the trees,
The squirrels wear googles to catch a sweet breeze.
They gather at night for a taffy delight,
While fireflies serve popcorn in a glowworm's light.

A raccoon with glasses reads tales of great glee,
As owls chuckle softly, sipping honeyed tea.
The mushrooms all dance in their polka-dot shoes,
While crickets compose songs of whimsical blues.

Wishing wells whisper, "Take a chance on a song,"
As frogs leap around, croaking, "Life's never wrong!"
Every shadow's a giggle, every path is a smile,
In this soft-glowing wonder, let's stay for a while.

So gather your sillies and bring them along,
In this glow-in-the-dark land, we'll all sing our song.
With every sprightly step and every cheerful huff,
We find that the magic is laughter enough.

Gardens of the Longing Heart

In a garden where flowers wear hats made of cheese,
Bees debate politics while buzzing with ease.
Sunflowers waltz in their tall, jaunty stance,
While turtles play chess, taking silly romance.

The daisies all giggle, exchanging their dreams,
Planting seeds of laughter beside babbling streams.
A gnome on a pogo stick sets off quite a scene,
As squirrels take selfies and make a magazine.

With every sweet bloom, a new joke takes flight,
As butterflies chuckle, joining in the delight.
The tomatoes are blushing; they think they're so cute,
In this garden where whimsies take root and reboot.

Let's toast with our rainbows and dance through the dirt,
Where gardening antics bring joy without hurt.
For in this vibrant patch, life isn't a chore,
Just laughter and love and a sprinkle of more.

The Elysian Chill

At a cool café made of whipped cream and fun,
We sip coconut lattes beneath a bright sun.
The tables float high, with chairs made of fluff,
Where every sweet pastry giggles enough.

The ice cubes are dancing in glasses of cheer,
While fruit hats wander around, spreading good cheer.
A candy cane waiter takes orders with flair,
And jellybean singers perform in midair.

The breeze whispers secrets of joyful delight,
As cookies and brownies win compliments bright.
With laughter as sprinkles on top of each thrill,
We savor our moments, embraced by the chill.

So come join the laughter, don't miss out the fun,
In this whimsical place, we laugh 'til we're done.
For every little sip gets sweeter with each laugh,
In the Elysian vibe, we find our own path.

Where the Ocean Meets the Sky

In a boat made of spaghetti, we sail,
With jellyfish dancing, we laugh and wail.
The seagulls in hats, so debonair,
Order pizza from their cloud in midair.

A dolphin jokes with a walrus, quite bright,
As we slip on the waves, feeling just right.
With sunscreen on our noses, looking so fine,
The sun starts to set, we sip on our wine.

Where the sea meets the sky, we twirl and we spin,
Life's just a game, let the laughter begin.
With flip-flops that squeak, and drinks full of fizz,
We toast to the horizon, it's all just a whiz!

So here in this moment, we savor the fun,
With stars peeking out, our day's almost done.
Underneath a blanket of shimmering gold,
Laughing at how life never gets old.

The Lure of Celestial Gardens

In gardens where cupcakes bloom like wild flowers,
We skip through the frosting for hours and hours.
Butterflies made of candy flit by,
Giggles and sprinkles float up to the sky.

With gnomes that tell jokes, it's a riotous scene,
They chuckle and dance in their berry-bush green.
We plant laughter seeds, watch them sprout,
In a patch where the silliness never runs out.

The rain is just chocolate, it falls with a cheer,
And sunbeams are marshmallows, oh how they appear!
With each gust of wind, the sweet scents collide,
It's not just a garden, it's a joyride!

In this place full of giggles, we catch all the bliss,
With tea brewed from laughter, oh, do take a sip!
As the moon gives a wink, we shout with delight,
In these celestial gardens, we'll dance through the night.

Chasing the Edge of Bliss

We sprint on the sand with our ice-cream cones,
Racing the waves, as we laugh and moan.
The beach balls are bouncing, the sun's like a cat,
It lounges and purrs, "Now how 'bout that?"

Kites painted like whales dance high up in the air,
With jokes on the strings that lead us somewhere.
We chase after giggles, they run and they hide,
While sandcastles sing with a humorous pride.

The tide rolls in softly, like jokes shared at night,
Under stars that chuckle, all twinkling and bright.
With a seagull as our DJ, it spins on a shell,
We dance on the shoreline, all wrapped in our spell.

Chasing the edge, where the laughter spills free,
With bubbles and sunshine, we shout with glee.
Tomorrow we'll find all the fun that we missed,
Together we'll laugh at the joys that persist.

Echoes of a Sunlit Utopia

In a land where the sun wears a silly bright hat,
We giggle at clouds that look just like a cat.
With rainbows of flavor swirling in the breeze,
We dance with the shadows and wiggle our knees.

The monkeys wear glasses, sipping fruit punch divine,
While parades of pink flamingos ooh and align.
With every explosion of giggles around,
The echoes of laughter are beautifully found.

Up high in the trees, where the bubbles do float,
A squirrel juggles nuts, what a talented goat!
With laughter resounding throughout every lane,
This sunlit utopia drives worries insane.

So let us collect every chuckle and cheer,
For in this sweet echo, there's nothing to fear.
With joy on our faces, we bask in the light,
In a world filled with nonsense, everything's right!

Shores of Infinite Possibility

On distant sands where seagulls play,
Sunburned folks sipping drinks by the bay.
With beach balls flying in a silly way,
Who knew sunburns could lead to a day?

Flip-flops flapping, laughter rings clear,
As the ice cream melts, it's a funny affair.
People dance with jellyfish in cheer,
A comedy show hosted by a crab near!

The Radiance Beyond the Waves

With waves that shimmer like disco lights,
We dodge the splash and laugh at our sights.
Someone's hair's a bird, taking off in flight,
Oh! That's just Dave with his new hair rights!

Sunhats wobbling, and tides that tease,
Crabs in tuxedos join our grand spree.
We sip on drinks filled with fizzy glee,
As the dolphins dance, proclaiming, 'Whee!'

A Journey to Tranquil Realms

On a boat made of gumdrops, we sail away,
Chasing rainbows, not a care in the fray.
Unicorns as crew, oh what a display,
Fish wearing bow ties join us for the play!

Navigating jellybean clouds up high,
We laugh so loud, our troubles say goodbye.
An octopus juggles, oh my oh my!
In this wacky trip, let the silliness fly!

Beneath the Canopy of Dreamscapes

Under trees where gummy bears grow,
We picnic with laughter, a sweet kind of flow.
A squirrel in shades puts on quite the show,
While taffy clouds float, putting sugar in tow!

In this land of fluff, let's dance like we're mad,
With pineapples wearing hats, it's not so bad.
A parade of kooky, we're all a bit rad,
In a realm of giggles, how lucky we've had!

Reveries in the Jewel of Dusk

As twilight paints the skies so bright,
I spotted a cat wearing a kite.
It danced on the breeze, what a sight to see,
Chasing its dreams, just like you and me.

A turtle in shades lounges by a stream,
Sipping on tea, living the dream.
A parrot cracks jokes, oh my, what a fuss,
While fireflies giggle, their glow a plus.

The stars join the party, twinkling with glee,
A raccoon provides snacks—who's got the fee?
Laughter rings out as the night takes flight,
In the jewel of dusk, all feels just right.

So bring out the joy, let your worries cease,
With critters around, who needs inner peace?
Life is a chuckle, a bright, silly ruse,
Under the twilight, it's hard to refuse.

Where the Sky Meets Serenity

A cloud floats by, sporting a hat,
Joined by a mouse with a big, squeaky spat.
They trade silly stories, all puffed up with pride,
While the sun peeks through, trying to hide.

Fish in the sea are learning to dance,
In sequined swimsuits, they twirl in a trance.
A dolphin does somersaults, quite the grand show,
While seagulls drop snacks—oh where did they go?

A pelican juggles, what a sight to behold,
With each fish that flies, another tale told.
Laughter erupts, as the sky bends with glee,
In this whimsical world where spirits roam free.

So here's to the sky, with its moments so bright,
Where silliness reigns in the fading light.
Forget your troubles, join in the fun,
In this realm of laughter, we're all number one.

Timeless Wonders of the Overlook

On the edge of a cliff, a wise old crow,
Tells tales of mishaps, his antics on show.
With a wink and a flap, he dives into the breeze,
Laughing at squirrels who spill all their cheese.

The flowers gossip, their petals all wide,
About a frog that wears roller skates with pride.
He zooms down the path, a blur of green joy,
While ladybugs giggle at every ploy.

In the shadows, a hippo plays peekaboo,
With a bunch of wild geese that honk just for you.
Bubbles of laughter, the air filled with cheer,
As fireflies weave stories, each one held dear.

Timeless it seems, this whimsical spree,
Where nonsense and joy blend so easily.
So come to the overlook, join the delight,
In the wonders of joy, everything feels right.

Horizon's Embrace of Promise

At dawn's early light, a squirrel runs fast,
Chasing shadows that never can last.
He stumbles and tumbles, a comic ballet,
While the sun bursts forth to brighten the day.

Fish toss their scales like glittering charms,
While the wind whispers sweet, silly alms.
A dog finds a hat and struts with a flair,
Wearing it proudly, oh what a rare affair!

As kites fly above, they twist and they spin,
A goat with a grin lets the mischief begin.
Each tug of the string brings giggles to air,
In this lovely farce, there's magic to share.

So dance with the breeze, let your heart be free,
Life's a funny stroll through the grand jubilee.
To the horizon we race, with a skip and a laugh,
In a world bright with joy, we're all part of the path.

Blossoms of Another World

In a garden where cats wear hats,
And squirrels dance like acrobats,
Flowers giggle, swaying bold,
Trading tales of dreams untold.

The bees do the cha-cha, oh so spry,
While butterflies pretend to fly high,
Bunnies sip tea with sugar and cream,
In this land where nonsense reigns supreme.

Clouds wear shoes that squeak and hop,
As rainbows twist and spin and flop,
Each butterfly is a tiny knight,
In a world where laughter takes its flight.

So pack your bags for this cartoon,
Bring your spoon and a cheerful tune,
For in this realm of silliness grand,
Joy awaits, just take my hand.

Calling of the Voyager's Dream

On a ship made of marshmallow fluff,
Sailing waves that are ever tough,
Captain Seal with a big green hat,
Navigates by the stars and a chat.

Octopuses juggle, it's quite a sight,
While the moon winks, illuminating night,
Fish wear tuxedos, elegant and neat,
As they host a ball with tap dance feet.

The compass spins with a playful glee,
Pointing to places we'll wait and see,
With every wave, a giggle erupts,
As seabirds tease with wobbly flaps.

Join this voyage, leave your cares,
Where laughter lingers and joy declares,
In a place where dreams make us beam,
And fun is the fuel for every dream.

Secrets of the Sunlit Horizon

There's a land where clouds taste like pie,
And the sun wears sunglasses, oh so spry,
Trees whisper secrets of silly things,
As they sway with joy in the breeze that sings.

Mountains wear hats that spin around,
While rivers giggle, bubbling sound,
Butterflies hold debates on the best,
Flavor of nectar to drink at a fest.

Tickling winds blow whispers bold,
Of socks that dance and stories told,
The stars come out to play a game,
Of hide and seek, oh what a claim!

So let's find this silly, shining space,
Where laughter blossoms in a warm embrace,
For the secrets here are sweet and bright,
In a world where humor takes its flight.

The Wish Upon a Radiant Wave

On a wave that twirls like crazy,
With seagulls pulling trick or maybe,
A wish is tossed as the tide rolls in,
For mischief bubbles, let the fun begin!

Shells giggle softly, sharing their look,
While crabs read poetry from a book,
The sand tickles toes with an honest tease,
As jellies wiggle with a joyful breeze.

Flip-flops chatter as they dance the night,
And starfish share jokes that feel just right,
In the glow of moonbeams swimming free,
Where laughter waves like the shining sea.

So toss your dreams upon this splash,
And let them soar in joy, a flash,
For in this land of whimsy and gleam,
Life is simply one big funny dream!

Celestial Journeys Await

A spaceship made of jelly beans,
Zooming past the flying machines.
With every bump we bounce and shake,
The cosmos giggles, make no mistake.

Stars in pajamas, sleeping tight,
Wishing on comets that took flight.
We wave at aliens, say 'hello!',
While munching popcorn, stealing the show.

Through asteroid fields, we twist and twirl,
Dodging space dogs in a galactic whirl.
Galaxies spin like a dizzying ride,
With laughter echoing far and wide.

Finally landing on a donut-shaped star,
We feast on sprinkles, oh so bizarre.
A cosmic party where all is bright,
Who knew the universe could be so light?

A Tapestry of Forgotten Dreams

Once I dreamed of flying high,
On a taco shaped like a pie.
But each gust of wind said 'not today!',
And I plopped down with a cheesy 'hayyy'.

Canvas of wishes now faded and torn,
Crafted by messes since I was born.
With wishful stitches on a wobbly seam,
I laugh at the chaos of each little dream.

Giraffes in top hats dancing with glee,
Whispering secrets that only they see.
Though my dreams might flicker and sway,
They still make me chuckle, come what may.

In this absurd quilt, there's joy in the fray,
As I tumble through life, come what may.
With friends like these, who needs a map?
Let's take a break for a silly nap!

The Horizon's Gentle Embrace

At dawn, the sun wears a cake-top hat,
Dancing with shadows on a friendly mat.
Seagulls sing songs of mischief and fun,
While waves tickle toes under the rising sun.

Clouds pinch and giggle, casting their shade,
As piña coladas in hand are laid.
Flip-flops lost in a sandcastle war,
While flip-flops laugh from the sandy floor.

Kites soar high, like dreams on a string,
Tugging at hearts, making spirits sing.
We chase the horizon with each silly skip,
On this delightful, carefree trip.

With laughter as bright as a sunlit bay,
Every glance shared makes shadows play.
We'll bottle this joy and let the world see,
That silliness is what sets us free.

Skylines Brushed with Velvet Dreams

The city sleeps in a fluffy robe,
Under stars that glitter like they stole the globe.
Skyline giggles peek through the mist,
Whispering secrets, can't resist.

Velvet cushions in clouds up high,
Tickle my fancy, oh me, oh my!
As pigeons perform their silly ballet,
I lose my hat in a gust of play.

Each light that twinkles is a wink from above,
Sending sweet giggles and dreams to love.
We draw doodles on the moon's soft face,
In this silly, nighttime embrace.

Chasing these visions 'til the morning dew,
With sassy stars cheering, 'You go, boo!'
At dawn we'll giggle, reminiscing the night,
Of skyscrapers dancing in soft starlight.

Threads of Destiny Unraveled

A cat in shades sits on the fence,
Deciding if this is worth the expense.
With fishy dreams, he takes a leap,
While mice below just plot and creep.

A dog in a suit prances around,
Chasing his tail, lost but not bound.
He barks at clouds, oh what a sight,
Yet slips on a banana peel, in mid-flight!

A parrot delivers the morning news,
Squawking loudly, forgetting the snooze.
With jokes that tickle the morning sun,
Every giggle wraps the day in fun.

So, laugh with abandon, let joys entwine,
In this silly realm where we're all fine.
For destiny's threads just twist and twirl,
In the humor of life, we happily whirl.

Whispers of a Dreamland

In a land where socks leave the dryer,
A unicorn grazes, looking for fire.
He flicks his mane with a comical flair,
While fairies giggle at his unkempt hair.

Clouds shaped like popcorn float on by,
Pigs in sunglasses zoom across the sky.
They snort with laughter, oh what a show,
As rain begins falling in caramel flow.

Children dance with ice cream cones,
Around a fountain of magical tones.
Each scoop a melody, sweet delight,
In whispers of dreams, they spin 'til night.

So let your heart wear a goofy grin,
For in this place, all the fun begins.
And in the silly, let laughter gleam,
In the whispers of a fanciful dream.

Beyond the Golden Dusk

Balloons float high, tied to a kite,
While squirrels are plotting to steal a bite.
With nutty bravado, they aim for the prize,
As cakes roll past, to everyone's surprise.

A snail in a top hat takes a slow twirl,
Chasing confetti, making a whirl.
The sun dips low, paints the sky bright,
As giggling stars prepare for the night.

Ticklish trees sway with the breeze,
As jokester flowers dance with ease.
A rabbit in slippers hops with glee,
In this realm where silly is key.

So join the fun in this sunset show,
Where laughter reigns and dreams overflow.
In colors of joy, let spirits rise,
As twilight sings under playful skies.

Echoes of a Distant Eden

A chicken crossed the road just to say,
"Why not have a dance party today?"
With roosters jammin' and hens on the floor,
They boogie and wiggle, oh, what a score!

A fish rides a bike through a garden of peas,
Wearing a helmet that barely fits, please.
He freestyles past veggies, shapes all around,
As carrots cheer on with a hop, then a bound.

Clouds rain jellybeans, sweet on the tongue,
While trolls in the corner sing songs and are young.
With jokes sharper than a wizard's wand,
They summon giggles, of which we are fond.

So come laugh aloud, let mischief unfold,
In this realm where magic never grows old.
With echoes of joy, let the good vibes mend,
In this humorous land, where all troubles end.

A Tapestry of Wandering Dreams

In a land where socks go missing,
And the ants throw a tea party's bliss.
Clouds are shaped like cats and kings,
While squirrels belt out tunes, oh what a twist!

Across fields of marshmallow fluff,
We dance with shadows, oh so spry.
The sun wears shades, looking quite tough,
And rainbows are just a wink from the sky.

A tree trunk sings a silly song,
While butterflies trade their jokes with glee.
In this realm, we endlessly belong,
With laughter that floats as light as a pea.

So grab your dreams, let's float away,
To a land where whimsy never ends.
We'll giggle about clouds all day,
And let the silly magic transcend.

Dreamscapes Beyond the Gloom

When shoes can talk and giggle too,
And coffee spills all over the floor.
We sail on boats made out of goo,
With jellyfish as our trusty oars!

In a world where cats play hopscotch,
Dancing to tunes of a quirky band.
Eggplant pirates squabble and watch,
As pancakes flip, a foodie's grandstand!

The moon is a giant smiling pie,
While the stars swing from threadlike beams.
We chase our hats as they fly high,
In this land where nothing's as it seems.

Let's frolic in clouds of cotton candy,
And share our giggles with the breeze.
In the realm of dreams, oh so dandy,
Where silliness hums with such ease!

Where Joy and Light Intertwine

In jungles of lollipops and dreams,
The rivers flow with fizzy drink.
We ride on ducks with feathery beams,
While talking flowers create a link.

Giggling fairies play hopscotch with tunes,
While silly creatures juggle bright suns.
Balloons float high like silly balloons,
As everyone plays and just runs!

Umbrellas made of pastels float high,
While laughter bubbles, a sweet serenade.
Bikes roll on clouds, watch the world fly,
In this place where light never fades.

So tap your feet and catch a smile,
Join the parade of candy delights.
In a dance that lasts all the while,
Where the fun sparks joy on starry nights!

Temptations of the Distant Shore

On the beach where sandcastles sigh,
Seagulls wear hats, quite ludicrous.
They squawk at the waves saying hi,
While crabs throw frisbees, oh so famous!

Corn on the cob dances the twist,
While jellyfish samba, moving in waves.
We sip on smoothies from coconut mist,
And ride on the backs of friendly knaves.

The sun throws confetti, what a sight,
While fish wear sunglasses, oh so neat!
Shells echo giggles, pure delight,
As we chill out to the ocean's beat.

So grab your floaties, it's time to play,
In the sun-soaked world, let's dive right in.
Where joy and laughter create a buffet,
Filled with memories waiting to begin!

The Promise of Sunlit Shores

When the sun gives a wink, the waves start to dance,
You'd think that the reef joined in on the prance.
Flip-flops are flying, someone just tripped,
Who knew a beach day could be so equipped?

Seagulls are screaming, demanding their share,
Of hot dogs and chips tossed up in the air.
We laugh till we ache, our sunscreen a mess,
Who knew sunbathing could lead to distress?

A crab named Maurice has stolen my snack,
He scuttles away—my sandwich! Attack!
And amidst all the chaos, a kid in a float,
Screams, "Look, I'm a dolphin!" but sinks like a boat!

At sunset we gather, our laughter and cheer,
The tide pulls our troubles far from our sphere.
Tomorrow we'll return, with gear and more snacks,
But tonight, just a nap—snoring's on our tracks!

Beneath Sapphire Skies

Beneath blue expanse, we lay like a rug,
One's snoozing, one's counting, that bug on a jug.
The sun beats down hot, turning folks to fried eggs,
While I over here hide, plotting sunburned legs!

With laughter erupting like fizz from a can,
The sun-kissed beards whisper, "Hey, where's the tan?"
We chase after kites, send toys soaring high,
Only to watch them crash, oh me, oh my!

My ice cream's a river, sliding down my shirt,
While friends crack up laughing, their faces all hurt.
Why does soft serve love to make such a mess?
Is it part of the gig? A creamy excess?

Yet, as stars appear 'neath the deepening blue,
With jokes that we share, the skies still feel new.
Tomorrow awaits with its mischievous grin,
But for now, we just chuckle—let the fun begin!

Journey to the Celestial Haven

Our backpacks are stuffed with dreams and with snacks,
We'll trek to the hills, dodging all of life's cracks.
The map is a puzzle, oh where do we go?
With twists and with turns, like a wibbly show!

I spotted a deer, shouted, "Look, the great king!"
But turns out it's just a lost puppy in Spring.
With giggles erupting like popcorn in heat,
We march through the trails, dodging mud with our feet!

The clouds start to gather, oh, the weather's quite bold,
"Frogs might just start dancing!" one brave friend foretold.
But rain brings the puddles, oh joy, what a treat!
Just don't step on that one—the squish is not sweet!

At last, we arrive where the stars kiss the land,
With smiles and wild tales—this was all we had planned.
Our journey is silly, but so full of cheer,
In this quirky adventure, we find all we hold dear!

Canvas of Celestial Vistas

Brushes in hand, we paint a great sky,
With pink, green, and orange—why not give it a try?
Our canvas is wobbly, like a table forlorn,
While squirrels come to check on our masterpiece born!

One's feet are now painted—who needs them anyway?
We'll leave little footprints to brighten the day!
As our colors collide like jellybeans on toast,
The palette's a party, let's raise up a toast!

"Wait, what's that splatter?" a friend starts to squeal,
"A more artistic drip, that's the new 'signature feel'!"
We chuckle at blunders, no reason to pout,
Every splash that we make is what it's about!

When the sun dips low, we admire our work,
A rainbow of joy—a colorful perk!
As giggles resound on this canvas so bright,
We're painting our joy with pure delight!

Soft Echoes of the Leeward Winds

The breeze giggles, tickles my chin,
A rogue kite swoops down, takes off with my grin.
Coconuts roll like a crowd in a stampede,
Chasing sunbeams and ice cream dreams at lightning speed.

Lizards in sunglasses lounge on the sand,
Sipping on juice, looking ever so grand.
Parrots strike poses, dramatically loud,
While clumsy crabs burst forth, drawing a crowd.

Seashells whisper secrets from shores of delight,
As a clam nearly trips—what a comical sight!
Frolicking waves crash, burst into laughter,
Leaving footprints of joy in their playful after.

With each gust that's breezy, the laughs unravel,
In this quirky wonderland where silliness travels.
Drinking in sunbeams, dancing 'til night,
In this merry land, everything feels right.

The Call of the Infinite Wave

Come ride the wave that giggles and sighs,
With dolphins who dance under cotton candy skies.
A fish gave a wink, with a wink back at me,
In a raucous pool party, how wild can we be?

Surfboards like surfboards, some less than afloat,
With sharks that wear helmets, insisting to vote.
The tide takes a selfie, a splash from a shell,
As the octopus juggles, oh do tell, do tell!

Jumping from foam, with squeals of pure glee,
A crab in a tutu—oh, what a sight to see!
Seashells tell jokes, or at least try to,
While the seagulls laugh loud, yes a crazy crew!

With a surf of pure joy and endless delight,
The waves roll on in a comical height.
So grab your board and feel the sun's spark,
In the laughter of oceans, we're never in the dark.

Boundless Blooms of the Evening

Flowers in hats say, 'We're ready for cheer!'
Bees buzzing loudly, 'This party's right here!'
The daisies are dancing, the tulips take flight,
In this garden so silly, all feels just right.

Bumblebees boogie to the pheromone beat,
See how the roses sway, moving their feet!
Fireflies whisper, 'Was that a pun upon?
Or just the petals' giggle at every dawn?'

A cactus is cracking a joke at the sun,
Saying, 'Prickly humor's just part of the fun!'
Ladybugs wink as they twirl in the night,
With giggling blooms, everything's bathed in light.

The moon takes the stage in a shimmering gown,
As flowers all cheer in their colorful crown.
So welcome the dusk with laughter and glee,
In this happy bloom village, don't bother to flee!

Faraway Skies and Silent Shores

Clouds like marshmallows drift on the breeze,
Waves whisper softly, begging for cheese.
Seagulls make puns as they dive for a snack,
While the tide rolls in, giving jokes a whack.

Sandy castles rise, topped with seashell gold,
Where clowns made of crabs put on shows bold.
Each seagull's a critic, judging the scene,
As the sun brings a smile to the beauty unseen.

Dunes where the tumbleweed rolls as it may,
Tickling the toes of the kids who just play.
Footprints of laughter, they dance in a line,
In the sun-soaked expanse, everything's fine.

As the horizon beckons with quirky delight,
We celebrate silliness, day turns to night.
Join in the fun where laughter won't die,
In these faraway moments, under wide-open sky.

Whispers of a Distant Eden

A squirrel in a tux, oh what a sight,
Dancing with the flowers, all day and night.
He thinks he's the king, with nuts in his bowl,
While the sun starts to giggle, it's got a role.

The stream sings a tune, slightly off-key,
And frogs in top hats add to the spree.
A picnic of ants, they brought tiny cheese,
With a weather report that says it's all breeze.

Clouds wear big shoes, prancing across,
While daisies in shades show off their gloss.
A rabbit with swagger, he hops with delight,
Chasing after dreams, till the fall of the night.

So if you hear laughter, don't be surprised,
In this distant Eden where joy's never disguised.
Every critter has jokes, and they're always on cue,
In a land full of giggles, just waiting for you.

The Promise of Sunlit Shores

A crab on a surfboard, feeling so cool,
Riding the waves, like it's some kind of school.
Seagulls in sunglasses, they squawk with flair,
Teaching the pelicans how to style their hair.

Beach balls are bouncing, and so is a cat,
Wearing a sunhat, it's a sight—imagine that!
Buckets of laughter rolling back to the shore,
While clam chowder jokes are never a bore.

Turtles in flip-flops move at their pace,
While fishes are playing a game of base race.
The sun's turned the sparkle to a glittery show,
When umbrellas start dancing, it's time for the flow.

So grab all your buddies, don't forget to bring snacks,
For the shore's full of treats and a few fun attacks.
In a place where the waves just giggle and sway,
Laughter's the treasure that brightens the day.

Dreams Woven in Golden Light

A snoring old bear, on a quilt made of cheese,
While rabbits knit sweaters that tickle the breeze.
Each stitch a little giggle, each loop a sweet dream,
In a garden where buttercups burst at the seam.

The moon flips pancakes, with syrupy grace,
While critters round up for the breakfast race.
A baker of clouds serves up pastries of air,
With flavors of laughter, they almost seem rare.

A firefly sings ballads, glimmering bright,
Telling tales of adventures that dance through the night.
While butterflies waltz, their wings all alight,
In dreams woven softly, where all feels just right.

So close your tired eyes, drift off to the glow,
Where the sweet taste of humor makes time move slow.
In a land full of wonders, funny and bright,
Every giggle's a treasure, glimmering in sight.

Beyond the Veil of Endless Skies

A cow in a rocket, beyond all the stars,
Sipping on moon milk, and chatting with Mars.
She giggles at comets, as they twirl and glide,
While astronauts join her, on this hilarious ride.

A parade of the planets, spinning with glee,
Where saturn's rings twinkle like blinged-out c's.
The sun wears a bowtie, feeling quite spry,
With clouds dancing gently, floating on by.

The stars throw a party, with snacks from the night,
Where wishes are whispered, and dreams take flight.
A constellation juggles, making magic with light,
In a universe funny, where all feels just right.

So if you stare up, and hear laughter above,
Know it's the cosmos giving all of its love.
For beyond every veil, and high in the skies,
Lies a world full of humor, where joy never dies.

In Search of Lost Serenities

I chased a cloud on roller skates,
It winked and giggled, oh what fun!
A rainbow laughed at my clumsy fate,
Said, "You look like you're on the run!"

I asked a star for some advice,
It blinked at me, 'You're doing fine!'
The moon played tricks, a game of dice,
And offered cheese with a side of wine!

I'll find that bliss, or so I vow,
With jellybeans and bubblegum,
Where golden cows just say, 'Moo wow!'
And everything is always fun!

So here I roam with a grin so wide,
In fields where giggles bloom at night,
With silly dreams I'll take in stride,
And dance until the morning light!

The Light Between Here and There

There's a glimmer on the lamp-lit way,
Where sock puppets throw a grand parade,
Lollipops promise to always stay,
While squirrels debate the best ice cream shade.

I waved at clouds that giggled back,
They tossed confetti from up so high,
One asked me if I owned a snack,
I said, "Only pizza to share, oh my!"

The sun, it twirled, a jester bold,
With sunbeams like silly string galore,
In the land of laughter, dreams unfold,
Where crickets sing and seagulls score!

So let's light hop to that joyful spot,
Where shadows play and giggles gleam,
Life's a joke we've all forgot,
And laughter's truly the best theme!

Fragments of a Perfect Tomorrow

I found a slice of cake in the grass,
Two squirrels danced, a lively pair,
They offered me a cup of sass,
And said, "Join us without a care!"

The sun was stuck in a disco ball,
While clouds were doing the cha-cha slide,
A froggy chorus began to call,
"Hop to it!" they croaked with pride!

Tomorrow's fragments shine so bright,
With jigsaw pieces made of cheese,
Each giggle adds a spark of light,
I'll take a dip in joyful seas!

So let's construct this whimsydome,
With bouncy castles, and rainbow pies,
In dreaming hearts, we'll find our home,
Where laughter greets the morning skies!

Portals to Vibrant Daydreams

I opened up a door to fun,
It giggled as I stepped right through,
Where jellyfish play a game of run,
And time flies by on a magic shoe!

The trees told stories, oh what sights,
With roots that dance and branches sing,
A hedgehog juggled stars at nights,
And butterflies wore crowns like kings!

Rainbows popped like bubbly tea,
While rain helped paint the skies anew,
It whispered tales of what could be,
Where silly dreams come chasing you!

So let's leap into this wonderland,
On marshmallow clouds we'll soar and play,
With goofy giggles hand in hand,
We'll dance till we're old and gray!

www.ingramcontent.com/pod-product-compliance
Lightning Source LLC
Chambersburg PA
CBHW072220070526
44585CB00015B/1419